DANCE ★ CRAZY

Quickstep

DANCE ★ CRAZY

Quickstep

Paul Bottomer

LORENZ BOOKS
NEW YORK • LONDON • SYDNEY • BATH

This edition published in 1997 by Lorenz Books
27 West 20th Street, New York NY 10011

LORENZ BOOKS are available for bulk purchase
for sales promotion and for premium use.
For details, write or call the manager of special sales:
Lorenz Books, 27 West 20th Street,
New York NY 10011; (800) 354-9657

Lorenz Books is an imprint of
Anness Publishing Limited

ISBN 1 85967 393 7

Publisher: Joanna Lorenz
Senior Editor: Lindsay Porter
Photographer: John Freeman
Stylist: Jackie Holland
Hair and Make-up: Karen Kennedy
Designer: Siân Keogh

Printed in China

1 3 5 7 9 10 8 6 4 2

Contents

Introduction

The Quickstep is one of the two most popular International Standard ballroom dances, along with the Waltz, although its origins are far from the respectable world of the ballroom. Allegedly, the dance owes its existence to the American vaudeville comedian Harry Fox, who worked American burlesque theaters just prior to World War I. At that time, the regulations regarding theatrical performances prohibited semi-clad female performers from moving on stage, and required them to remain in fixed poses in "artistic" tableaux. Fox hit upon the idea of performing a little dance movement around the statically-posed women in between jokes. This feature grew to be such an integral part of his act that it became his hallmark as his fame and popularity spread. The popular music industry of the time, affectionately known as Tin Pan Alley, was quick to exploit the potential of Harry Fox's Trot and was soon promoting the music and steps of the "Foxtrot."

The dance was characterized by a slow walk taking two beats of music and a series of quick steps, or trots, each taking a single beat of music. Initially, the Foxtrot relied heavily upon moves from other dances such as the One-step and the Rag, but teachers soon began to show their ingenuity by creating new figures to meet the demand. By 1915, not only had the Foxtrot reached England, but it had soared to new heights of popular acclaim. At this point in the story of the Quickstep, its Foxtrot forerunner was danced at a tempo of about 32 bars per minute, but in 1916 dancers started to adapt the dance to slower music with a more gliding feel. To differentiate it from the usual, quicker Foxtrot, this slower Foxtrot was initially called the Saunter, and it was this dance that later laid the basis for the beautiful Slow Foxtrot.

By the end of World War I, jazz was coming into its own, expressing the post-war mood of liberation. In the 1920s, the tempo of life quickened, as did the pace of the now jazzed-up Foxtrot. By the mid-1920s, dance bands were frequently playing the Foxtrot at a rapid 50 bars per minute – the Quick Foxtrot. To contend comfortably with such a pace, the dancers were forced to rise to their toes so the quick steps were danceable. The craze showed no signs of flagging, and then, in 1925, the

Left: With its lively tempo, the Quickstep is now one of the most popular ballroom dances.

Charleston appeared. While extremely popular as a fad dance, the Charleston lacked long-term potential. However, it was not long before the dance was being adapted, and in 1927 it was combined with the Quick Foxtrot, resulting in a dance with the tediously lengthy name: Q.T.F.T & C. – the Quick Time Fox Trot and Charleston. The Charleston fell into decline, but its influence lived on in the Q.T.F.T & C., now sensibly renamed the Quickstep.

Throughout the 1930s and 1940s, the Quickstep's lively and vivacious character embraced the big band swing sounds. In the 1950s, 1960s and up to the present, there have always been plenty of foot-tapping tunes and romantic up-tempo melodies for which the Quickstep was the natural dance choice. While the tempo has gradually come down from the athletic 54–56 bars per minute set in 1929 to a pleasant 48–50 bars a minute for social dancing in the 1990s, the Quickstep has lost nothing of its verve and lust for life.

At its most advanced, the Quickstep is now a uniquely satisfying combination of body swing movements and syncopated hops, danced at a speed at which the dancers can feel the breeze in their hair. At its most social, the dance offers a relatively easy to learn and repeatable basic pattern that everyone can enjoy. With the instructions on the following pages, we hope you will take your partner in your arms and ease into the rhythm and swing of what has become the classic Quickstep.

Music

Quickstep music is organized with four beats to each bar of music. The first and third beats are both accentuated by the musicians, but the first beat is stronger. It is on the first strong beat that you will take your first step of the dance. You will become familiar with counting the steps of the moves in "Quicks" and "Slows." A "Quick" equates to a single beat of music, while a "Slow" equates to two beats. Most of the basic moves in the Quickstep start with a "Slow" count followed by two "Quick" counts. Some, like the Quarter Turn to the Right, are then completed with another "Slow" count, while others, such as the Natural Turn, have a different rhythm. Note that because both the first and third beats are accentuated, you will not necessarily complete a move in a single bar of music. The Quarter Turn to the Right with a count of "Slow-Quick-Quick-Slow" will take 1½ bars of music, while a Natural Turn with a count of "Slow-Quick-Quick-Slow-Slow-Slow" will take 2½ bars of music. You need not be consciously aware of this while you are dancing; it is sufficient to be aware of the "Slows" and "Quicks" of the steps you are dancing.

Musically, the time signature of the Quickstep is 4/4 with a tempo currently recommended internationally at 50 bars per minute, although, for social dancing, Quicksteps can be enjoyed at tempos ranging from 48 to 52 bars per minute. This tempo is a little faster than a brisk walking pace but can seem very fast indeed to start with. However, as you increase your familiarity with the Quickstep and remember to take small steps as you dance, the momentum of the moves themselves will help you cope with the tempo.

On the Floor

The floor is primarily for the benefit of the dancers – it is not a thoroughfare. Always walk around the edge of the floor and never across it, especially while people are dancing. The sudden emergence of a bystander trying to dodge dancers can cause chaos on the floor and is an unnecessary hazard to the dancers.

When taking to the floor, it is important to avoid causing problems for the dancers who are already there. Since men normally start a dance facing the outside of the room, it may seem quite natural for them to walk onto the floor backward while their attention is focused on their partner. As this could cause a hindrance to the other dancers, it is much better to approach the floor and assess the flow of floor traffic before taking up your starting position, with due consideration for the dancers on the floor.

When leaving the floor, especially during the course of a dance, the same consideration to the other dancers should be shown. If you are finishing during the dance, you should dance to the edge of the floor, leave the floor at that point and walk around the perimeter to your seat.

Basic Floor Craft

While you and other dancers are dancing around the floor, you should be aware of other couples and their likely direction of travel. Knowing how to avoid problems is a great advantage to a dancer, and ways of doing this are described in the Floor Craft sections later in the book. There are, however, a few general rules worth mentioning now.

• It makes sense for more experienced dancers to give way to less experienced couples.

• If you see a potential problem, you should take action to avoid it. Usually the couples farther back in the flow of floor traffic have the best perspective.

• Never dance across the center line of the room into the oncoming flow of floor traffic.

With a little practice, the ability to avoid dancing into a problem will itself yield satisfaction and enjoyment.

The Dance Floor

Before you begin learning the dance steps, here are some basic ways of orienting yourself in the room.

• The flow of the floor traffic (the dancers) will be in an overall counterclockwise direction around the room.
• In the Basic Quickstep, progression around the room is achieved by making a series of moves along the dance floor using a pattern which travels between zigs and zags.
• The orientation of the dancers during the moves will be described in relation to the nearest wall, the center line of the floor and in terms of zigs and zags.

GOING WITH THE FLOW
Assuming the room is rectangular, stand adjacent to any wall, making sure the wall is on the man's right and the woman's left. The man will now be in position to move forward with the flow of floor traffic and the woman to move backward.

THE CENTER LINE
Still in the same position, the center line of the room will be on the man's left and the woman's right.

ZIGS AND ZAGS
A diagonal line, which we will call a "zig," extends from the center line to the wall parallel to it at an

Right: The diagram illustrates the main ways in which the dancers orient themselves in the room. You can start to get used to this by practicing at home.

angle of approximately 45°. Another diagonal line, a "zag," extends from the wall to the center line at an angle of approximately 45°. In the Basic Quickstep, the man moves forward along the zigs and backward along the zags in order to "tack" along the room. Conversely, the woman moves backward along the zigs and forward along the zags, opposite her partner, as they both travel with the flow. Remember that as you dance around the room, you will encounter corners.

CORNERING
When you turn a corner, you will orient yourself using the new wall and the new center line, which is always parallel to the wall you are using. The zigs and zags run along the diagonals between the new center line and the new wall, as before. The flow will, of course, flow right around the corner.

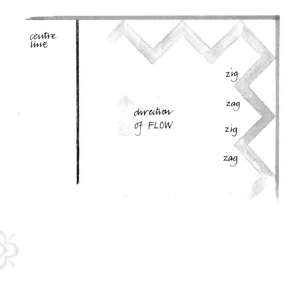

The Hold

When taking up a hold, the man takes the woman's right hand in his left hand and draws her to him. This enables him to place the woman in the best position for dancing, which is with the woman standing slightly to his right. When in the correct position, the buttons on the man's shirt should be opposite the woman's right shoulder.

To take up the hold, the man presents his left hand as if he is a policeman stopping traffic. The woman then places the hooked middle finger of her right hand between the thumb and forefinger of the man's left hand, palm to palm. Next, the woman places her forefinger and third finger on top of her middle finger, rests her little finger on top of the others and curls her thumb around the man's thumb. The man now places the fingertips of his left hand along the edge of the woman's right hand with the fingers pointing to the floor. In this way, the underside of both the man's left wrist and the woman's right wrist are facing the floor. When you start to dance, this will considerably enhance stability and make leading much easier.

The man then cups the woman's left shoulder blade with his right hand, with the fingertips placed against the woman's spine. The woman straightens the fingers of her left hand but allows the thumb to extend out in its natural position. She then places her left hand on the man's upper arm with a straight and flat wrist. It is unnecessary for her third and little fingers to be resting on the man's arm. Both the man and the woman should hold their elbows slightly forward from their backs and a little away from the body. They should relax the shoulders.

The man and woman should both stand upright, lifting the diaphragm to produce good posture. They should hold their heads a little to the left and with their chins up. The weight of the head is such that it can have an adverse effect on balance if it is not held in the desired position. Do not look at your feet. The man's back and arms provide a "frame" in which the woman is held. A good frame is essential for good dancing and good leading.

Far left: The hold (front view)

Left: The hold (rear view)

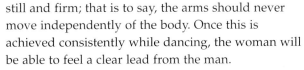

Leading and Following

The hold and starting position often feel too rigid to a first-time dancer for fluidity of movement, but with a little practice, a good but relaxed posture and hold can be developed. This is one of the main skills that characterize a dancer who is easy to dance with. The frame created by the man's arms and reinforced by his back and diaphragm should be held

still and firm; that is to say, the arms should never move independently of the body. Once this is achieved consistently while dancing, the woman will be able to feel a clear lead from the man.

Much of the process of leading is not something the man does actively but rather is the result of skillful and effective dancing. The best leading is that which simply leaves the woman with no other option but to dance what the man intends without her really having to think about it. Once the woman has to work at following, the enjoyment of the dance is largely lost for her. The woman should accept the man's lead and not try to guess what he will do next, because she could commit herself too soon to a course of action that might be the wrong one. Under no circumstances should the woman ever try to lead the man, especially when he is trying to learn a new figure. It is impossible for a man to learn and work things out for himself while at the same time trying to react to his partner's leading.

The woman has a particular responsibility when she is moving forward and the man is moving backward. Since she is the one who can see where the couple is moving, she must indicate to the man if they are about to dance into a problem. She can do this by squeezing the man's upper arm between the thumb and middle finger of her left hand and then allowing him to lead his evasive maneuver.

Right: This position shows the frame, created by the man's arms. The arms, back and diaphragm all move with one another – no element moves independently. This provides the frame with which to lead the woman.

Far right: The woman indicates strategical problems with a slight pressure of the left hand.

Legs and Feet

It may seem surprising to save comments on the legs and feet until last. However, we dance with our whole bodies, and once the body is working properly, the feet and legs will often largely take care of themselves. Knees are very important, and you will feel more comfortable, relaxed and in control if you can keep your knees flexed at all times. Dancing, in a basic sense, is not so very different from walking, and yet it is common that someone who can walk perfectly well will feel challenged when taking a normal walk forward, simply because they are "dancing" and not walking down the street.

WHICH FOOT TO START WITH

Some teachers teach the Quickstep by starting with the man walking forward onto the left foot. Logic suggests that when we are moving forward and want to initiate a turn to the right, we do this by curving the right foot forward. This is a good move to start with because the woman will feel the curve and instinctively will know that, because she is moving backward, she should start moving directly back with her left foot. If the man were to start with his left foot moving forward and to dance without turning, the woman would not have such a clear lead.

Above and right: When taking a step, move your foot into position and then remember to move your body weight directly onto that foot.

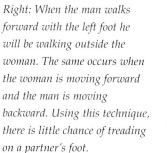

Left: Try not to get too far away from your partner or worry about stepping on his or her feet. As the woman is positioned slightly to the man's right, when he walks forward with the right foot his foot will go between the woman's feet.

Right: When the man walks forward with the left foot he will be walking outside the woman. The same occurs when the woman is moving forward and the man is moving backward. Using this technique, there is little chance of treading on a partner's foot.

Basic Quickstep

The Basic Quickstep described here consists of two sections: a forward half and a backward half. Both halves travel along the room in an overall counterclockwise direction, with the flow. The side-close-side movement in Steps 2–4 of both halves of the Basic Quickstep is known as a "chassé" (pronounced "sha-say"). Start in the hold described earlier, with the feet together and standing about 4 ½ feet away from the edge of the floor to allow sufficient space to dance into. The man is ready to move forward along a zig and the woman to move backward along it.

FORWARD HALF – *Quarter Turn to the Right*

1 Man
Walk forward with the right foot along the zig, starting to turn to the right.
(Count – slow)

1 Woman
Walk back with the left foot along the zig, starting to turn to the right.
(Count – slow)

2 Man
Move sideways onto the toes of the left foot, traveling along the room but facing the wall.
(Count – quick)

2 Woman
Move sideways onto the toes of the right foot, traveling along the room but facing the center line.
(Count – quick)

3 Man
Close the toes of the right foot to the toes of the left foot, continuing to turn to end on the zag, backing the center line of the room. (Count – quick)

3 Woman
Close the toes of the left foot to the toes of the right foot, continuing to turn to end on the zag. (Count – quick)

4 Man
Walk back along the zag toward the center line, lowering toe-heel onto the left foot. (Count – slow)

4 Woman
Walk forward along the zag toward the center line, lowering toe-heel onto the right foot. (Count – slow)

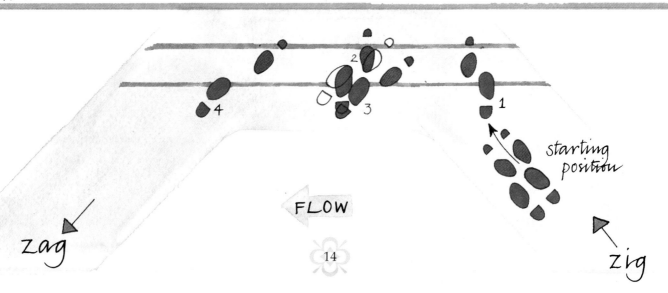

WALL

FLOW

zag

zig

starting position

BACKWARD HALF – *Progressive Chassé*

1 Man

Walk back along the zag with the right foot, moving toward the center line and starting to turn to the left. (Count – slow)

2 Man

Move sideways onto the toes of the left foot, traveling along the room and pointing the left foot along the zig. (Count – quick)

1 Woman

Walk forward along the zag with the left foot, moving toward the center line and starting to turn to the left. (Count – slow)

2 Woman

Move sideways onto the toes of the right foot, traveling along the room and turning a little to the left to end with your back square to the wall. (Count – quick)

3 Man

Close the toes of the right foot to the toes of the left foot. End facing the zag. (Count – quick)

3 Woman

Close the toes of the left foot to the toes of the right foot, continuing to turn to the left to end backing along a zig. (Count – quick)

4 Man

Move sideways, lowering toe-heel onto the left foot to end pointing along the zig. (Count – slow)

4 Woman

Move sideways, lowering toe-heel onto the right foot. (Count – slow)

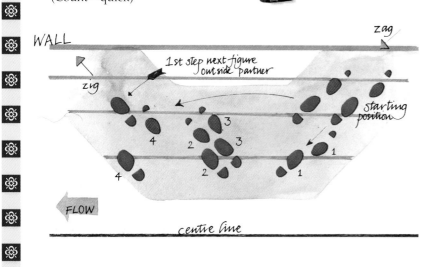

You can now repeat the Basic Quickstep with one important difference. On each subsequent Step 1 of the Basic Quickstep or other following move, the man will walk forward with his left foot outside the woman's right side. The woman's steps remain the same.

Rise and Fall

Rise and fall is the elevation and lowering that the dancer feels as he or she moves onto the toes of a foot and then relaxes through the knee, ankle and toes to end on a flat foot. Rise and fall will therefore take the dancer both above and below normal height. In reality, rise and fall is a by-product of the natural swing of the Quickstep, giving the dance the speed and flow that have ensured its liveliness and continuing appeal. A good swing action is something that dedicated competitors strive to achieve over many years of rigorous coaching and strenuous practice. Social dancers can also introduce rise and fall and start to enjoy the improved feeling and appearance of their dance by following a few simple guidelines.

Left: A walk forward on Step 1 will usually be a normal walk, staying down, though starting to rise at the very end of the step as the body weight rolls over the toes.

Left: On the last step of the bar, whether that is Step 3 or 4, the dancer will usually lower toe-heel onto the flat foot.

Right: A move to the side on Step 2 will usually lift onto the toes.

• *Generally, the dancers will walk, either staying down or lowering on a slow count.*

• *Most "Quick" counts are danced on the toes.*

Right: On figures with four steps in one bar of music, for example, a Chassé, the dancer will rise more gradually over the first three steps before lowering gently on the fourth using a toe-heel action.

Natural Turn around a Corner

In all the standard dances, including the Quickstep, special figures have been devised to help dancers turn around a corner. Here is one of the easier ones, which will help you to flow easily around the corner and leave you in exactly the right position to continue dancing the Basic Quickstep along the new wall. Start having danced the Basic Quickstep. The man is standing on his left foot ready to move forward toward the wall along a zig and the woman is standing on her right foot ready to move backward along the zig.

NATURAL TURN

1 Man
Walk forward along the zig with the right foot, outside the woman's right side and starting to turn to the right.
(Count – slow)

2 Man
Move sideways along the zig onto the toes of the left foot, continuing to turn to the right. (Count – quick)

1 Woman
Walk back along the zig with the left foot, starting to turn to the right.
(Count – slow)

2 Woman
Move sideways along the zig onto the toes of the right foot, continuing to turn to the right.
(Count – quick)

3 Man

Close the toes of the right foot to the toes of the left foot and lower onto the right foot, turning to face against the flow. (Count – quick)

3 Woman

Close the toes of the left foot to the toes of the right foot and lower onto the left foot, turning to face with the flow. (Count – quick)

AROUND A CORNER

4 Man

Walk back with the left foot, continuing to turn to the right and releasing the right toes from the floor but keeping the heel in contact with it. (Count – slow)

4 Woman

Walk forward with the right foot, continuing to turn to the right. (Count – slow)

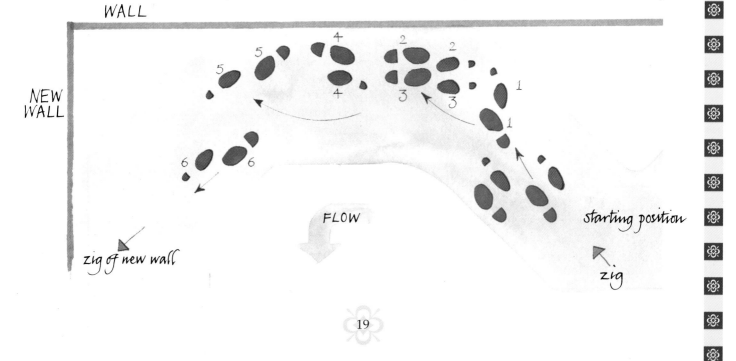

WALL

NEW WALL

FLOW

zig of new wall

starting position

zig

19

5 Man

Pull the right foot back with the heel in contact with the floor, then slide the foot around, continuing to turn to end facing along the zig of the new wall, with the right foot to the side of the left foot and with feet apart. (Count – slow)

6 Man

Walk forward with the left foot along the zig of the new wall. (Count – slow)

5 Woman

Move sideways onto the left foot, continuing to turn to the right to face the wall. (Count – slow)

6 Woman

Walk back with the right foot, continuing to turn to the right to move back along the zig of the new wall. (Count – slow)

Natural Turn with Hesitation

This is a useful variation of the Natural Turn, which can be danced near the beginning or middle of a wall and which combines well with other figures described later in the book. Start by dancing the first three steps of the Natural Turn around a Corner.

1–3
Dance steps 1–3 of the Natural Turn around a Corner

4 Man
Walk back with the left foot, continuing to turn to the right and releasing the right toes from the floor but keeping the heel in contact with it.
(Count – slow)

4 Woman
Walk forward with the right foot, continuing to turn to the right.
(Count – slow)

5 Man
Pull the right foot back with the heel in contact with the floor, then slide the foot around to end to the side of the left foot, with feet apart. Continue turning to the right to end facing along the zag toward the center line.
(Count – slow)

5 Woman
Move sideways onto the left foot, staying down with flexed knees and continuing to turn to the right to end on the zag facing the wall.
(Count – slow)

6 Man

Slide the left foot to close to the right foot but remain standing on the right foot. (Count – slow)

6 Woman

Slide the right foot to close to the left foot but remain standing on the left foot. (Count – slow)

Continue with the Progressive Chassé to the Right, the Chassé Reverse Turn or the Quick Open Reverse Turn, which are described later in the book.

Sway

Sway is rather like the banking of a motorcyclist travelling around a bend in the road. It is an important feature of a nice, easy and relaxed style. When dancing a section of Quickstep that has only three steps in the bar, for example, a walk-side-close movement during a turn, it is quite natural for the body and head to tilt or sway a little away from the reaching foot to act as a counter-balance. Natural sway will occur on Steps 2–3 of the Natural Turn, to the right for the man and to the left for the woman. Sway is therefore an essential feature of balancing comfortably as you dance.

Floor Craft

Your positioning on the floor and how you progress around it may be likened to driving in a flow of traffic. The skill, experience and thinking ahead necessary to negotiate the other traffic on the dance floor are known as floor craft.

As you get used to dancing the Basic Quickstep and the Natural Turn around a Corner, it will become apparent that there is more to floor craft than is at first obvious to the casual observer. The ability to avoid problems and to read the situation ahead develops with practice but can be acquired more easily by following a few guidelines, the responsibility for which lies mainly with the man.

• It is extremely important to adhere to the given orientation in the room. If you allow yourself to wander from the prescribed path, it will be very difficult to get back to it.

• If you are following a couple around a corner, stay behind and on the wall side of them. By the time you reach their position, they will usually have moved on.

• Avoid dancing across a corner if a couple is already in the corner. You risk being run into as they exit the corner.

• Women, even though they may wish to help, should not attempt to lead the man.

All the figures described in this book have been selected not only for their attractiveness as easily enjoyable figures but also for their usefulness and practicality as floor craft figures. As your repertoire grows, so will your ability first to avoid problems and then to escape any further difficulties.

When you first try out your Quickstep at a dance, you will find that one of the man's main preoccupations will be to avoid other dancers as you progress around the floor. Sometimes, split-second decisions have to be made to avoid bumping into another couple. It is therefore important that the man leads the woman by making his intentions very clear. He should not and need not physically maneuver the woman if he dances his chosen move with clarity.

Right: The man must give a clear lead to the woman, and the woman must not try to anticipate the man's movements.

Natural Spin Turn

In dancing terminology, "natural" simply refers to a move that turns to the right. You have already danced the Natural Turn around a Corner and it is now time to try another figure, which has become the international standard way of cornering in the Quickstep. Start by dancing Steps 1–3 of the Natural Turn around a Corner. The man is facing against the flow with his feet together and standing on his right foot. The woman is facing with the flow with her feet together and standing on her left foot.

1–3

Dance steps 1–3 of the Natural Turn around a Corner.

4 Man

Move back onto the left foot, turning it inward to make a strong turn to the right. Keep your knees together. (This will feel awkward at first but only because you are dancing it step by step. At normal speed, the move will flow much more comfortably.) (Count – slow)

4 Woman

Move forward onto the right foot, turning strongly to the right to end backing the zig of the new wall. Keep your knees together. (Count – slow)

5 Man

Walk forward between the woman's feet onto the right foot on the zig of the new wall and lift up onto the toes of the right foot. Continue turning to the right on the toes of the right foot, keeping the left foot behind. (Count – slow)

5 Woman

Move back onto the toes of the left foot on the zig of the new wall, continuing to turn to the right. Bring the right foot back out of the way to touch the left foot. (Count – slow)

6 Man

Relax back onto the left foot away from the corner, having turned onto the zag of the new wall.
(Count – slow)

6 Woman

Move forward, toward the center line, lowering onto the right foot on the zag of the new wall. (Count – slow)

Note that the feet do not close. Continue by dancing straight into the Backward Half of the Basic Quickstep, the Progressive Chassé.

 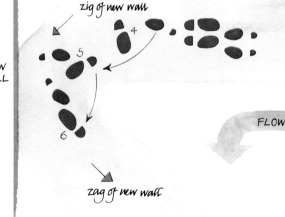

Practical Tip

Some men find it helpful to think of Steps 4–6 as a rock back, a rock forward lifting and a rock back, while remembering, of course, to turn. It is a common error for the man to make Step 5 a side step (shown below).

Dance Tip

When dancing this figure, it is important for the man to keep his head to the left throughout the figure.

Lock Step

You can now dance a continuous Basic Quickstep with either the Natural Turn or Natural Spin Turn at the corners. The Lock Step will complete your repertoire of International Standard Basic Quickstep figures. The name is a little misleading as the feet cross only loosely and do not actually "lock." The steps are the same for both the man and the woman. While the man dances the Forward Lock Step, the woman dances the Backward Lock Step, and vice versa. Dance this figure after the Basic Quickstep as a useful spacer for improving your positioning prior to dancing one of the corner figures. It can also be inserted between two groups of the Basic Quickstep. As you dance the Lock Step, imagine a line parallel to the wall and dance along it.

FORWARD LOCK STEP – *Start facing the zig, with feet apart and standing on the left foot. Throughout this move, remain facing along the zig but traveling along the line parallel to the wall.*

2 Walk forward onto the toes of the left foot along the line. (Count – quick)

1 Walk forward with the right foot, outside your partner's right side onto the line parallel with the wall. (Count – slow)

Double Lock Step

For a classy combination of the Lock Step that will add sparkle to your Quickstep, steps 2 and 3 can be repeated before continuing into step 4. This is called the Double Lock Step.

3 Still on the toes of the left foot, cross the right foot loosely behind the left foot.
(Count – quick)

4 Walk forward along the line, lowering onto the left foot. (Count – slow)

WALL

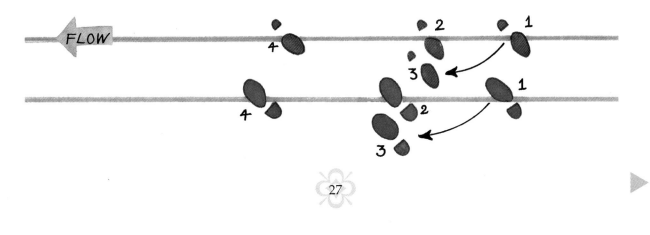

FLOW

BACKWARD LOCK STEP – *Start backing the zig, with feet apart and standing on the right foot. Throughout this move, remain backing along the zig but traveling along the line parallel to the wall.*

1 Walk back with the left foot onto the line parallel with the wall. (Count – slow)

2 Walk back onto the toes of the right foot along the line. (Count – quick)

3 Still on the toes of the right foot, cross the left foot loosely in front of the right foot. (Count – quick)

4 Walk back along the line, lowering onto the right foot. (Count – slow)

Fitting the Basic Quickstep into the Room

As you dance the Basic Quickstep, you may well find that when you want to dance the Natural Turn or the Natural Spin Turn at a corner you are not quite in the right position. As a general rule, it is much better to dance the corner figure early, as the later option could see you disappearing off the edge of the floor. With practice, however, there will no longer be a danger of this as you will be able to gauge your progression around the room so that you arrive near the corner in a perfect position to dance around it.

In the Quickstep, the length of the steps should never be increased to the point where the figures and

movement become distorted. It is much better to adjust the angles of the zigs and zags during the Basic Quickstep. A greater amount of turn will result in more progression along the floor and a lesser amount in less progression. In addition, figures such as the Lock Step can be used to extend a Basic Quickstep by half as much again to help put you in the right position. Be aware that less experienced dancers often try to dance an extra Basic Quickstep when really they ought to have started the corner figure. This error often results from the dancer not having planned ahead sufficiently, so it is important to start thinking about the corner as soon as you have danced about halfway along the room.

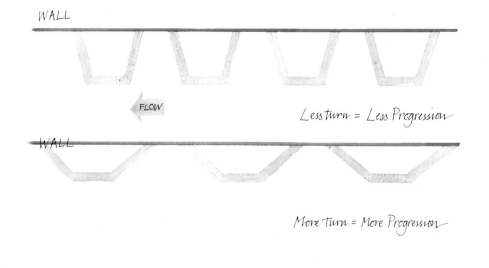

WALL

FLOW

Less turn = Less Progression

WALL

More Turn = More Progression

Natural Hairpin and Running Finish

Imagine you are on a zig ready to dance the Basic Quickstep or the Lock Step and the way ahead of you is not clear. Now is the time to dance the Natural Hairpin and conclude it with a very stylish flowing movement called the Running Finish, which can also be used later with other figures.

NATURAL HAIRPIN

1 Man
Walk forward with the right foot, curving it outside the woman's right side onto the zig, and start turning to the right.
(Count – slow)

1 Woman
Walk back with the left foot, starting to curve to the right.
(Count – slow)

2 Man
Move forward onto the toes of the left foot, continuing to curve strongly to the right. (Count – quick)

2 Woman
Move back onto the toes of the right foot, continuing to curve strongly to the right.
(Count – quick)

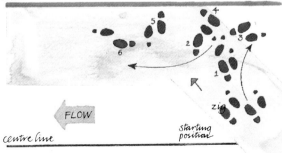

WALL

FLOW

centre line

4

5

2

3

6

1

zig

starting position

Style Tip

To help your turn, see how the man will bank or sway to the right and the woman to the left on Steps 2–3.

RUNNING FINISH – *The Running Finish can also be danced after Steps 1–3 of the Natural Turn or the Natural Spin Turn. At a corner, simply go with the flow and bend the Running Finish around it.*

1 Man
Move back along the zig under your body, starting to turn to the right. (Count – slow)

3 Man
Walk forward, lowering onto the right foot, slightly across yourself and outside the woman, continuing to curve to the right to end facing almost against the flow.
(Count – quick)

3 Woman
Take a small step back, lowering onto the left foot underneath your body and continuing to curve strongly to the right to end facing almost with the flow.
(Count – quick)

Timing Tip

Until you get the hang of this figure, Steps 2 and 3 can be danced as slows.

1 Woman
Walk forward with the right foot, outside the man's right side and turning to the right along the zig.
(Count – slow)

32

2 Man

Move sideways onto the toes of the right foot facing the center line and, still turning to the right, sway to the left. (Count – quick)

2 Woman

Move sideways onto the toes of the left foot facing the wall and, still turning to the right, sway to the right. (Count – quick)

3 Man

Swing your left side forward to face with the flow, swaying to the left, and move forward, lowering onto the left foot. (Count – quick)

3 Woman

Swing your right side back to face against the flow, swaying to the right, and take a short step back, lowering onto the right foot. (Count – quick)

Continue by dancing the Basic Quickstep with the man moving his right foot forward outside the woman on the first step and turning a little more than usual to resume the normal orientation. Alternatively, you can dance the Lock Step. For added style, try combining the Natural Hairpin, the Lock Step (Backward for the man, Forward for the woman) and the Running Finish, before resuming with either the Forward Lock Step (for the man) or the Basic Quickstep.

Chassé Reverse Turn

This is a short but useful figure that follows the Natural Turn with Hesitation described earlier. In dancing terminology, "reverse" simply refers to a turn to the left. It does not mean that the figure moves backward. The man is standing on his right foot and the woman on her left with the feet almost closed. The man is facing the center line along the zag and the woman is backing the center line along the zag.

1 Man
Walk forward with the left foot, along the zag toward the center line, starting to turn to the left. (Count – slow)

2 Man
Move sideways onto the toes of the right foot, continuing to turn to the left. Sway to the left. (Count – quick)

1 Woman
Walk back with the right foot, along the zag toward the center line, starting to turn to the left. (Count – slow)

2 Woman
Move sideways onto the toes of the left foot, continuing to turn to the left. Sway to the right. (Count – quick)

3 Man

Close the left foot to the right foot and lower onto the left foot. Continue to sway to the left and turn to end facing against the flow. (Count – quick)

3 Woman

Close the right foot to the left foot and lower onto the right foot. Continue to sway to the right and turn to end facing with the flow. (Count – quick)

Continue with the Progressive Chassé (the Backward Half of the Basic Quickstep) but turning it a little more than usual to resume its normal orientation.

Style Tip

The man will curve his left foot into this move to help lead the turn while the woman will ensure that she takes a shorter step on step 2 to help the man move around her. The important thing is to keep the flow moving through the turn and allow it to run out into the following chassé.

WALL

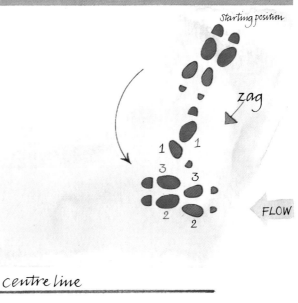

Starting position

zag

1   1

3   3

2   2

FLOW

centre line

Open and Quick Open Reverse Turns

Here are two alternatives to the Chassé Reverse Turn that enhance the flow of the dance and can still be enjoyed by less experienced dancers. The steps for each of the turns are the same. In the Open Reverse Turn, the count for each step is "slow," while in the Quick Open Reverse Turn, the count is as given below. Either of these moves can follow the Natural Turn with Hesitation.

1 Man
Walk forward with the left foot, along the zag toward the center line, starting to turn to the left.
(Count – slow)

1 Woman
Walk back with the right foot, along the zag toward the center line, starting to turn to the left.
(Count – slow)

2 Man
Move sideways onto the toes of the right foot, continuing to turn to the left. Sway to the left. (Count – quick)

2 Woman
Move sideways onto the toes of the left foot, continuing to turn to the left. Sway to the right. (Count – quick)

3 Man

Move back, lowering onto the left foot under your body and continuing to sway and turn to the left to end facing against the flow. (Count – quick)

3 Woman

Take a small step forward across yourself, lowering onto the right foot and continuing to sway to the right and turn to the left to end facing with the flow. (Count – quick)

> *Continue with the Progressive Chassé (the Backward Half of the Basic Quickstep) but turning it a little more than usual to resume its normal orientation.*

A New Combination

Part of the fun of dancing the Quickstep is enjoying different combinations and groups of figures. Here is one of the most popular combinations, loved by social dancers and often used by competitors:

• the Natural Spin Turn, danced along the side of the room

• the Progressive Chassé, moving sideways toward the center line

• linking step: the man walks forward and across himself with his right foot outside the woman's right side, while the woman walks back with her left foot (Count – slow)

• as the dancers move from the linking step into the Quick Open Reverse Turn, they should feel as though they are untwisting through the movement

• the Progressive Chassé, turned a little more than usual to end in its normal orientation.

Outside Change

This is another very simple figure but one that has a nice feel to it and will help add variety to your increasing repertoire of Quickstep moves. It is a good floor craft move, enabling you to overtake slower couples immediately ahead. In this move, the woman does not turn her body. This results in her ending in a slightly open or "promenade" position on Step 3. You can insert it into your program after Steps 1–3 of the Natural Turn or the Natural Spin Turn, having reduced the amount of turn ("underturned") a little so the man ends on a zag facing the wall. The man is standing on his right foot and the woman on her left. Both have their feet together.

1 Man
Walk back with the left foot along the zag. (Count – slow)

2 Man
Walk back onto the toes of the right foot, still on the zag, starting to turn to the left. (Count – quick)

3 Man
Take a small step to the side along the room by lowering onto the left foot to end facing the wall in Promenade Position, with the left foot pointing along the zig. (Count – quick)

3 Woman
Take a small step to the side along the room by lowering onto the right foot, pointing it down the room and moving your head to the right to end in Promenade Position. (Count – quick)

1 Woman
Walk forward with the right foot. (Count – slow)

2 Woman
Walk forward onto the toes of the left foot. (Count – quick)

Continue with the Chassé from Promenade Position.

Promenade Position

Promenade Position is a frequently used position in standard dancing. It simply means that the couple has moved into a position in which the distance between the man's left shoulder and the woman's right shoulder is greater than the distance between the man's right shoulder and the woman's left. The couple is therefore slightly open on the man's left and the woman's right side. It is crucial that this very slightly open position is not exaggerated to become an almost side-by-side position. In the Promenade Position, the woman will be looking to the right and the man slightly further to the left than normal. When the man uses his right foot and the woman her left foot to take a step in

Promenade Position, it will be taken "through the middle" between the dancers and along the same line. Because of the relative positioning of their bodies, the man's foot will go through first. Such a step should be a short one to avoid distorting the top half of the body.

Left: In the Promenade Position the couple are slightly open on the man's left and the woman's right side. The couple should not over-emphasize the position or they will end up side by side.

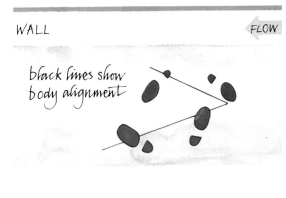

WALL

FLOW

black lines show body alignment

Chassé from Promenade Position

A Chassé is simply a side-close-side movement, and you have already danced this in the Basic Quickstep. Here, the Chassé is danced from the Promenade Position following the Outside Change. The dancers move along a line parallel to the wall but maintaining their zig alignment. In addition, the woman gradually moves her head to the left as she resumes her normal position facing the man.

1 Man
Take a short step forward and across yourself with the right foot, along the line. (Count – slow)

2 Man
Move onto the toes of the left foot, still progressing along the same line. (Count – quick)

1 Woman
Walk forward and across yourself with the left foot, along the line and starting to turn to the left. (Count – slow)

2 Woman
Move sideways onto the toes of the right foot, along the same line and continuing to turn to the left. (Count – quick)

3 Man
Close the toes of the right foot to the toes of the left foot.
(Count – quick)

4 Man
Move sideways, lowering onto the left foot along the same line to end on the zig. (Count – slow)

3 Woman
Close the toes of the left foot to the toes of the right foot, completing the turn to face the man.
(Count – quick)

WALL

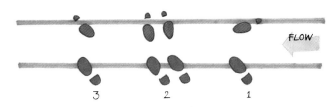

FLOW

3   2   1

4 Woman
Move sideways, lowering onto the right foot, along the same line to end on the zig. (Count – slow)

> *Continue into the Basic Quickstep, the Natural Turn around a Corner or the Natural Spin Turn, remembering that on Step 1 of the next figure, the man will walk forward with the right foot outside the woman.*

Hover Corté

The Hover Corté is a superb and elegant floor craft figure that you can dance immediately after the Forward Half of the Basic Quickstep (the Quarter Turn to the Right) if your path into the Backward Half (the Progressive Chassé) is blocked. The man is standing on his left foot and the woman on her right, with feet apart.

1 Man
Walk back along the zag with the right foot, starting to turn to the left. (Count – slow)

2 Man
Move sideways onto the toes of the left foot, turning onto the zig and swaying to the right. (Count – slow)

3 Man
On the zig, lower your body weight sideways onto the right foot. (Count – slow)

1 Woman
Walk forward along the zag with the left foot, starting to turn to the left. (Count – slow)

2 Woman
Move sideways onto the toes of the right foot, turning onto the zig and swaying to the left. (Count – slow)

3 Woman
On the zig, lower your body weight sideways onto the left foot. (Count – slow)

Having successfully avoided the problem on the dance floor, continue as follows on the next page.

4 Man
Walk back with the left foot, moving temporarily against the flow. (Count – slow)

5 Man
Move sideways onto the toes of the right foot, swaying to the left. (Count – quick)

6 Man
Standing on the toes, close the left foot to the right foot and lower onto the left foot, still swaying to the left. End on the zig. (Count – quick)

4 Woman
Walk forward with the right foot, outside the man's right side and moving temporarily against the flow. (Count – slow)

5 Woman
Move sideways onto the toes of the left foot, swaying to the right. (Count – quick)

6 Woman
Standing on the toes, close the right foot to the left foot and lower onto the right foot, still swaying to the right. End on the zig. (Count – quick)

Continue into the Basic Quickstep, the Natural Turn, the Natural Spin Turn or the Natural Hairpin, remembering that on Step 1 of the next figure, the man will walk forward with the right foot outside the woman.

Hover Telemark

The Hover Telemark is a classic figure that is not only extremely useful but also has a superb look and feel and is not difficult to lead. The description of the moves needs to be carefully followed before success will be achieved. Dance this figure after the Natural Turn with Hesitation at a corner. A great option is to dance the Tipple Chassé around a Corner but with the man swaying to the left and the woman to the right and lowering on Step 4 before dancing straight into the Hover Telemark.

1 Man

Walk forward onto the left foot along the zig but turning your body to the left so that you feel you are almost walking across yourself. Relax the knees and look straight ahead along the zig.
(Count – slow)

1 Woman

Walk backward onto the right foot along the zig but turning your body to the left so that you feel you are almost walking across yourself. Relax the knees and turn your head well to the left as you feel the clear lead of this figure.
(Count – slow)

2 Man

Move forward along the zig onto the toes of the right foot, turning your body to the right so that it comes square with the feet. (Count – quick)

3 Man

Take a small step to the side along the room by lowering onto the left foot but pointing the left foot along the zig in a Promenade Position. (Count – quick)

2 Woman

Move back along the zig onto the toes of the left foot, turning your body to the right so it comes square with the feet. Move your head gradually over to the right, matching your body's rate of turn. At the end of the step, your head will be facing the man.
(Count – quick)

3 Woman

Take a small step to the side along the room by lowering onto the right foot but pointing the right foot along the room. Move your head over to the right to finish in a Promenade Position. (Count – quick)

Continue with the Chassé from Promenade Position.

Progressive Chassé to the Right

Following the Natural Turn with Hesitation, this figure can move you quickly and easily along the floor with the flow around the room. The Chassé, as usual, is danced along an imaginary line parallel to the wall.

1 Man
Walk forward onto the left foot, starting to turn to the left. (Count – slow)

2 Man
Move sideways along the line onto the toes of the right foot, continuing to turn to the left to end with your back square to the wall.
(Count – quick)

1 Woman
Walk back onto the right foot, starting to turn to the left. (Count – slow)

2 Woman
Move sideways along the line onto the toes of the left foot, continuing to turn to face the wall. (Count – quick)

3 Man

Close the toes of the left foot to the toes of the right foot, continuing to turn to the left to end backing along the zig. (Count – quick)

4 Man

Move sideways, still along the line, lowering onto the right foot. (Count – slow)

4 Woman

Move sideways, still along the line, lowering onto the left foot. (Count – slow)

3 Woman

Close the toes of the right foot to the toes of the left foot, continuing to turn to the left to end facing along the zig. (Count – quick)

> *You can now continue with a super-smooth ending: either dance the Backward Lock Step followed by the Running Finish or go straight into the Running Finish.*

V-6 Combination

When a figure combination becomes very popular, it often becomes a set piece in the dance. The V-6 combines the Backward Lock Step with a modified Outside Change. As the name suggests, the figure makes a "V" pattern, making it an ideal move to dance along the short side of the floor.

THE ENTRY – *Dance the Natural Spin Turn around the corner at the end of a long side and finish it with the man backing the new center line along a zag. Alternatively, dance Steps 1–3 of the Natural Spin Turn, starting on the short side (after a Natural Turn around a Corner) and underturning the move to 90° to end backing the new center line along a zag.*

Right: The V-6 entry with the man backing along a zag

BACKWARD LOCK STEP – *If you danced the Natural Spin Turn as the entry, now dance Steps 2–4 of the Lock Step (Backward for the man and Forward for the woman), moving toward the center line of the short side of the floor. If the alternative entry of Steps 1–3 of the Natural Turn has been used, then dance Steps 1–4 of the Lock Step (Backward for the man and Forward for the woman), with the woman taking her first step in line with the man.*

Left: The Lock Step, step 4

OUTSIDE CHANGE – *The Outside Change is now modified to fit the different context in which it is danced.*

1 Man
Walk back with the left foot underneath your body, along the zag. (Count – slow)

2 Man
Walk back onto the toes of the right foot, still on the zag and starting to turn to the left. (Count – quick)

1 Woman
Walk forward with the right foot outside the man's right side. (Count – slow)

2 Woman
Walk forward onto the toes of the left foot, starting to turn to the left. (Count – quick)

3 Man

Take a small step to the side along the room by lowering onto the left foot to end facing the wall, with the left foot pointing along the zig. (Count – quick)

LOCK STEP EXIT – *The best exit to this combination is for the man to dance the Forward Lock Step and the woman to dance the Backward Lock Step. The angle at the point of the "V" may be adjusted so the V-6 can be fitted exactly into the short side of many ballrooms. If you find that this is the case, you can return to your program by dancing into one of the corner figures, such as the Natural Spin Turn, remembering that the first step of the following figure for the man will be outside his partner. Otherwise, continue into the Basic Quickstep or a "natural" figure.*

3 Woman

Take a small step to the side along the room by lowering onto the right foot to end backing the wall. (Count – quick)

Summary of Counts for the V-6 Combination

Natural Spin Turn	Counts – Slow, Quick, Quick, Slow, Slow, Slow
Steps 2–4 of the Backward Lock Step (man) and Forward Lock Step (woman)	Counts – Quick, Quick, Slow
Modified Outside Change	Counts – Slow, Quick, Quick
Forward Lock Step (man) and Backward Lock Step (woman)	Counts – Slow, Quick, Quick, Slow

If the alternative entry is used, the count will be:

Steps 1–3 of the Natural Spin Turn	Counts – Slow, Quick, Quick
Steps 1–4 of the Lock Step	Counts – Slow, Quick, Quick, Slow

Tipple Chassé around a Corner

Now that you are building up a repertoire of useful and enjoyable figures, you can combine parts of the moves you already know with a new element in a popular and attractive group – the Tipple Chassé. This is a very flexible figure and, in the first combination, you can use it around a corner. Remember to allow sufficient room ahead of you to dance the figure. For the entry, start by dancing Steps 1–3 of the Natural Turn around a Corner or the Natural Spin Turn.

ENTRY – *The man is now facing against the flow with his feet together and standing on his right foot. The woman is facing with the flow with her feet together and standing on her left foot.*

1 Man
Walk back with the left foot, starting to turn to the right.
(Count – slow)

1 Woman
Walk forward with the right foot, starting to turn to the right.
(Count – slow)

2 Man
Move sideways onto the toes of the right foot, completing a 90° turn to the right to face with the flow along the new wall. Sway to the right and look past the woman's left shoulder.
(Count – quick)

2 Woman
Move sideways onto the toes of the left foot, completing a 90° turn to the right to face against the flow along the new wall and swaying to the left.
(Count – quick)

Style Tip

The man should dance this section taking small steps.

3 Man

Close the toes of the left foot to the toes of the right foot, still swaying to the right. (Count – quick)

4 Man

Move sideways onto the toes of the right foot, swaying to the right and turning onto the zig of the new wall. (Count – slow)

3 Woman

Close the toes of the right foot to the toes of the left foot, still swaying to the left. (Count – quick)

4 Woman

Move sideways onto the toes of the left foot, swaying to the left and turning onto the zig of the new wall. (Count – slow)

Variation

When you have practiced the standard Tipple Chassé, you can develop it further by introducing the Backward Lock Step for the man and the Forward Lock Step for the woman between the Entry and the Tipple Chassé. The woman must make some modifications to ensure that the move goes smoothly:

• take Step 1 of the Forward Lock Step in line with the man.

• take Step 1 of the Tipple Chassé outside the man's right side. The count for this Lock Step will be the usual slow, quick, quick, slow.

Continue along the zig of the new wall by dancing Steps 2–4 of the Forward Lock Step for the man and the Backward Lock Step for the woman. The man will move his left side forward and the woman her right side back as they move into the Lock Step.

Tipple Chassé along the Room

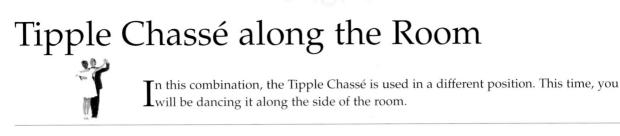

In this combination, the Tipple Chassé is used in a different position. This time, you will be dancing it along the side of the room.

ENTRY – *Dance the Progressive Chassé to the Right, followed by the Backward Lock Step for the man and the Forward Lock Step for the woman, along the zig.*

1 Man
Walk back with the left foot, starting to turn to the right. (Count – slow)

2 Man
Move sideways onto the toes of the right foot, turning to the right. Sway to the right and look past the woman's left shoulder. (Count – quick)

2 Woman
Move sideways onto the toes of the left foot, turning to the right and swaying to the left. (Count – quick)

1 Woman
Walk forward with the right foot, starting to turn to the right. (Count – slow)

> ## Style Tip
> The man should dance this section taking small steps.

3 Man

Close the toes of the left foot to the toes of the right foot, still swaying and looking to the right. (Count – quick)

4 Man

Move sideways onto the toes of the right foot, swaying to the right and turning onto the zig. (Count – slow)

3 Woman

Close the toes of the right foot to the toes of the left foot, still swaying to the left. (Count – quick)

4 Woman

Move sideways onto the toes of the left foot, swaying to the left and turning onto the zig. (Count – slow)

Continue by dancing Steps 2–4 of the Forward Lock Step for the man and the Backward Lock Step for the woman. The man will move his left side forward and the woman her right side back as they move into the Lock Step.

Swing

A good swing epitomizes the action used by expert dancers of the Quickstep. While in the early stages of mastering the Quickstep, you will not have much time to think about developing a good action; sooner or later you will want to enhance your enjoyment and improve your style with a little bit of swing. If you were to suspend a pendulum from the ceiling, then pull it back and release it to fall by the force of gravity, it would travel in an arc along a straight line. You can begin to use such a natural swing in your Quickstep. In most of the figures in standard dancing, swing acts on alternate sides of the body in each bar of music or set of three steps. Swing can be applied to any figure, and here the Natural Turn is used as an example.

Left: On Step 1, the man walks forward with his right foot along the zig.

Right: As the man turns to the right on Step 2, swing will act on his left side, causing him to rise and helping to propel his left side toward the wall faster than his right side, which has become the center of the turn.

Below: On Step 3, the swing naturally continues upward, taking the man's left side with it and causing him to turn and continue rising with the swing's momentum. When the dancer is turning, the swing action will also cause him or her to incline the body toward the center of the turn – this inclination is called "sway."

Right: Since swing occurs in a straight line, the feet also use that straight line. Steps 1–3 of the Natural Turn are all taken on the same line (in this example, on the zig), regardless of the turn and where the feet happen to be facing. On Steps 4–6, each step will be taken on the same floorboard or line parallel with the wall, while the swing will act on the man's right side.

Style Tip

When dancing with a swing action, Step 2, which is usually a side step, carries the powerful swing momentum and will therefore be longer than Steps 1 or 3.

Swing is responsible for maintaining a proportional amount of turn, alignment, rise and fall, footwork, sway and length of step in many Quickstep figures. Swing also leads to a less energetic and more economical way of moving. It is an important ingredient of good dancing and one that your local coach or dance school can help you continue to develop.

Figures and Combinations

The following tables suggest ways of combining the figures you have learned to create your own routines.

Figures starting with the man moving the right foot forward toward the wall on a zig.

- Quarter Turn to the Right
- Natural Turn
- Natural Turn with Hesitation
- Natural Spin Turn
- Forward Lock Step
- Natural Hairpin

Figures that can or do end in the Promenade Position.

- Outside Change
- Hover Telemark

Figures starting with the man moving the left foot forward toward the center line. on a zag.

- Chassé Reverse Turn
- Open and Quick Open Reverse Turns
- Progressive Chassé to the Right

Figures that can or do start from Promenade Position.

- Chassé from Promenade Position
- Natural Hairpin

PRECEDING AND FOLLOWING FIGURES

Quarter Turn to the Right

Preceding Figures:
Progressive Chassé
Natural Turn
Forward Lock Step
Running Finish
Chassé from Promenade Position
Steps 4–6 of the Hover Corté
V-6 Combination
Tipple Chassé

Following Figures:
Progressive Chassé
Hover Corté

Progressive Chassé

Preceding Figures:
Quarter Turn to the Right
Natural Spin Turn
Steps 1–3 of the Chassé
    Reverse Turn
Open and Quick Open
Reverse Turns

Following Figures:
Quarter Turn to the Right
Natural Turn
Steps 1–3 of the Natural Turn
Natural Turn with Hesitation
Natural Spin Turn
Forward Lock Step
Natural Hairpin
Tipple Chassé around a
    Corner

Natural Turn

Preceding Figures:
Progressive Chassé
Forward Lock Step
Running Finish
Chassé from Promenade
    Position
Chassé Reverse Turn ending
    with the Progressive
    Chassé
Open or Quick Open
    Reverse Turn ending with
    the Progressive Chassé
Steps 4–6 of the Hover Corté

Following Figures:
Quarter Turn to the Right
Natural Turn with
    Hesitation
Natural Spin Turn (along the
    room side)
Forward Lock Step
Natural Hairpin
    Steps 1–3 of the Natural
    Turn

Natural Turn with Hesitation

Preceding Figures:
Progressive Chassé
Forward Lock Step
Running Finish
Chassé Reverse Turn ending
with the Progressive Chassé
Open or Quick Open Reverse
Turn ending with the
Progressive Chassé
Chassé from Promenade
Position
Steps 4–6 of the Hover Corté

Following Figures:
Chassé Reverse Turn
Open or Quick Open
Reverse Turn
Progressive Chassé to the
Right

Natural Spin Turn

Preceding Figures:
Progressive Chassé
Forward Lock Step
Running Finish
Chassé Reverse Turn ending with the
Progressive Chassé
Quick Open Reverse Turn ending
with the Progressive Chassé
Chassé from Promenade Position
Steps 4–6 of the Hover Corté

Following Figures:
Progressive Chassé
Hover Corté
Progressive Chassé leading into the
Open or Quick Open Reverse Turn
V-6 Combination

Forward Lock Step

Preceding Figures:
Progressive Chassé
Forward Lock Step
Running Finish
Chassé Reverse Turn ending with the Progressive Chassé
Open or Quick Open Reverse Turn ending with the
Progressive Chassé
Chassé from Promenade Position
Steps 4–6 of the Hover Corté

Following Figures:

Quarter Turn to the Right	Natural Turn
Natural Turn with Hesitation	Natural Spin Turn
Forward Lock Step	Natural Hairpin
Tipple Chassé around a Corner	
Steps 1–3 of the Natural Turn	

Backward Lock Step

Preceding Figures:
Steps 1–3 of the Natural Turn
Backward Lock Step
Progressive Chassé to the Right
Natural Spin Turn (see the V-6 combination)

Following Figures:
Steps 4–6 of the Natural Turn
Steps 4–6 of the Natural Turn with Hesitation
Backward Lock Step
Running Finish
Tipple Chassé along the Room

Steps 1–3 of the Natural Turn:
This can be considered as a
move in its own right, as it
is frequently used as an
entry to other figures.

Preceding Figures:
As for the Natural
Turn

Following Figures:
Backward Lock Step
Running Finish
Outside Change
Tipple Chassé around a
Corner
V-6 Combination

Natural Hairpin

Preceding Figures:
Progressive Chassé
Forward Lock Step
Running Finish
Chassé Reverse Turn
ending with the
Progressive Chassé
Chassé from Promenade
Position
Steps 4–6 of the Hover Corté

Following Figures:
Backward Lock Step
Running Finish
Outside Change
V-6 Combination

Running Finish

Preceding Figures:
Steps 1–3 of the
    Natural Turn
Backward Lock Step
    (toward the wall
    along a zig)
Natural Hairpin

Following Figures:
 Quarter Turn to the Right
 Natural Turn
    Steps 1–3 of the Natural Turn
    Natural Turn with Hesitation
    Natural Spin Turn
 Forward Lock Step
    Tipple Chassé around a Corner

Chassé Reverse Turn

Preceding Figures:
Natural Turn with Hesitation
Backward Lock Step (toward the wall along a zig)
    followed by Steps 4–6 of the Natural Turn with
    Hesitation
Progressive Chassé to the Right followed by Steps 4–6 of
    the Natural Turn with Hesitation

Following Figures:
Progressive Chassé
Hover Corté (starting with the man facing against the
    flow and turned a little more than usual to resume the
    normal ending alignment, facing the wall along a zig)

Outside Change

Preceding Figures:
Steps 1–3 of the
    Natural Turn
    (ending with the
    man backing the
    center line along a zag)
Natural Hairpin

Following Figures:
Chassé from Promenade
    Position

Chassé from Promenade Position

Preceding Figures:
Outside Change

Following Figures:
Quarter Turn to the Right
Natural Turn
Steps 1–3 of the Natural Turn
Natural Turn with Hesitation
Natural Spin Turn
Forward Lock Step
Natural Hairpin
Tipple Chassé around a
    Corner

Hover Corté

Preceding Figures:
Quarter Turn to the Right
Chassé Reverse Turn

**Following Figures
(including Steps 4–6):**
Quarter Turn to the Right
Natural Turn
Steps 1–3 of the Natural
    Turn
Natural Turn with
    Hesitation
Natural Spin Turn
Forward Lock Step
Natural Hairpin

Hover Telemark

Preceding Figures:
Natural Turn with Hesitation (at the
    beginning of a new wall)
Steps 4–6 of the Natural Turn with
    Hesitation (at the beginning of a
    new wall)

Following Figures:
Chassé from Promenade Position

Progressive Chassé to the Right

Preceding Figures:
Natural Turn with Hesitation
Steps 4–6 of the Natural
    Turn with
        Hesitation

Following Figures:
Steps 4–6 of the
    Natural Turn
        with Hesitation
Backward Lock Step (toward
    the wall along a zig)
Running Finish

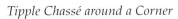

V-6 Combination

Preceding Figures:
There is a choice of two
   recommended entries to
   the V-6:
Steps 1–3 of the Natural Turn
Natural Spin Turn

Following Figures:
As for the Forward
   Lock Step

Tipple Chassé around a Corner

Preceding Figures:
Progressive Chassé
   Natural Turn
   Forward Lock Step
  Running Finish
Chassé from Promenade Position
Steps 4–6 of the Hover Corté
V-6 Combination

Following Figures:
Quarter Turn to the Right
Natural Turn
Steps 1–3 of the Natural Turn
Natural Turn with Hesitation
Natural Spin Turn
Forward Lock Step
Natural Hairpin

Tipple Chassé along the Room

Preceding Figures:
Progressive Chassé to the Right
   followed by the Backward
   Lock Step

Following Figures:
 Quarter Turn to the Right
   Natural Turn
    Steps 1–3 of the Natural Turn
     Natural Turn with Hesitation
     Natural Spin Turn
 Forward Lock Step
   Natural Hairpin
    Tipple Chassé around a
     Corner

QUICKSTEP

Additional Information

The following organizations will be able to provide you with
information about standard ballroom dancing in your area.

Fred Astaire International
407 Bloomfield Avenue
Verona, NJ 07044
(201) 239-1200

National Dance Council of America
P.O. Box 2432
Vienna, VA 22183
(703) 281-1581

North American Dance Teachers Association
P.O. Box 85
Vienna, VA 22180
(703) 938-2709)

Arthur Murray Dance Studios
677 Fifth Avenue, 4th Floor
New York, NY 10022
(212) 935-7787

Arthur Murray Dance Studios
262 North Beverly Drive
Beverly Hills, CA 90210
(310) 274-8867

Acknowledgments

*The author and publishers would like to thank the following for their
participation in this book:*

*Michael Burton, Elaine Bottomer, Julie Glover, Trevor and Naomi Ironmonger,
Tanya Janes, Camilla Laitala, Jeff and Teresa Lindley and Debbie Watson.*

*Dance shoes provided by Supadance International Limited
Evening dresses provided by After 6, Consortium, Tadashi and Vera Mont.*